DELIVERANCE FROM SELF

DELIVERANCE FROM SELF

BISHOP R. W. SIMMONDS

ONTARIO, CANADA, 2017

ISBN 9780995878754

Table of Contents

Dedication

This book is dedicated to the Holy Spirit Who leads and guides me, and to the Lord Jesus Christ Who has delivered me from the curse, the penalty and the bondage of sin. This book is also dedicated to all those who have stood with us in arriving at our present destination. Many people from all walks of life have helped us and we give God praise and thanks for bringing such individuals our way. Had it not been for God, Whose goodness and mercy has prevailed, we would not have arrived here and at this publication, for God's glory.

Acknowledgement

We acknowledge the works of God Almighty in every way. In all circumstances we say thank You, Father, for Your great goodness, love and mercy towards our life in this journey.

I acknowledge my wife, Pastor Claudette, who has stood with me through thick and thin for the 34 years that we have been married. I want to thank her for assisting me in writing this book.

To our children, Lamoi, Stacy-Ann, and Matthew, and our granddaughter, Jaharah, thank you for making us a family. Love you all dearly.

Special Thanks To:

Pastor Barbara Lindsay, Elder Clive Lindsay, Grace Restoration Ministries Int'l, Toronto

Deacon Winston and Ucolly Gray, Parents-in-law Bishop Michael Johnson, Miracle Centre Prayer Tower Ministries International

My related sisters and brothers.

Thank you all!

Foreword

Are you walking free outwardly, yet you are spiritually a prisoner of self? Is the jail sentence hanging on your neck and weighing heavily on you today? You are not alone. Millions of people you meet on the streets are walking about daily, yet they are serving a life sentence imposed by self. No matter how successful they seem, they are walking in chains and are in need of a deliverer and deliverance.

We have a Deliverer Who has finished the work at the Cross for us. We now have to identify the chains that bind us to the prison of self and allow the finished work of the Cross, to take our chains off.

The jail term is about to be overturned and all prisoners set free to fulfill the destiny for which they were created. The mandate and mission God has assigned to you is about to be unleashed. Are you prepared?

Walk with me through the pages of this book as we discover the prison sentences we are serving and the steps that will walk us to the full deliverance and freedom God desires for us.

"I am come that they might have life, and that they might have it more abundantly." (John 10:10)

Introduction

Let's start by saying that many of the problems each person goes through in his or her life are mainly due to the foundation of the family tree. This accounts for our last name, until we change it ourselves.

Our DNA is linked to the roots of the family tree; every lifestyle that we will ever begin to pursue finds its original roots in the family tree. When the roots are bad, the fruit will also be bad; by treating the roots, you will be able to alter the fruits.

Many times we want to treat the fruits and the branches of our lives but we forget that the roots, which the naked eye cannot see, are submerged under the years of iniquities, transgressions and sins of our forefathers.

If you come from a family with righteousness, the fear of God and order, your fruit will provide the evidence of this as you are of the same roots.

You always reap what you sow; forever, this will be. God has given you a chance and a choice on the road of your life to make amends and to turn in the right direction. Life is a game and we all have a choice in deciding how we play it to benefit ourselves and our generations down the road.

Chapter One:
The Battle Has Begun!

When you are born you come into the world with very little or no knowledge of your environment, as the spiritual realm is kept secret from the naked eye.

There are two worlds: the spiritual world and the physical world. Irrespective of what you believe, this is a fact of life. There are things that are hidden from the physical world which are in existence in the spiritual world. For example: no one can see the wind, yet it exists and produces an effect.

The physical and spiritual worlds have an effect on every single person. Both of these forces have an effect – directly and indirectly – against mankind.

Likewise, your DNA is affected by your environment, your belief system and the culture you belong to. The Bible tells us in Hosea 4:6 that by rejecting the knowledge of God's Word, we open ourselves up to suffering. Every person comes under the same condition. There are no exceptions.

Let us consider some key Scriptures which will help us to understand the battle that is before us.

The Greek word "EKBALLO" (Mark 16:11) means:

"eject, cast out demons (ekballo), drive out, expel, fire." Jesus cast out many demons and evil spirits of all kinds (Mark 1:34, Luke 4:41).

There are two key Hebrew words for deliverer. The first one is "NATSAL," which means, "to take away or snatch away riches, wealth and blessings" (Psalm 25:5, Psalm 25:20, 2 Chronicles 20:25). It also means "to spoil" (Exodus 3:22).

The second keyword is "PALAT" (Psalm 40:17). This is the other Hebrew word for deliverer. It means "to slip away or escape from the hands of obstacles." The Bible says, "The Almighty God is our great deliverer." (Psalm 18:12)

There are forces in the spiritual realm which work against or support each person, be it a blessing or a curse. You make a choice to activate blessings or curses to follow your life. The DNA of your original roots, as well as the subsequent behaviors of your own life, contributes to the outcome of your life.

We all have a choice to initiate blessing or curses, either by following the path of our original DNA from our family roots, or adopting a new one from the knowledge acquired through walking with God, and the study and meditation of the Word of God.

The Greek word "DAIMONIODES" (James 3:15) is the word "devilish, demonic or diabolical." Each person initiates their own demonic forces based upon their behavior with respect to the actions they carry out in life.

The Greek word "DIABOLOS" (Matthew 4:1) describes "adversary that throws fiery missiles (Ephesians 6:16)." It also means, "enemy, critic, liar (John 10:10), murderer and persecutor."

The word "MASHAL" (Psalm 8:6) is the Hebrew word for, "dominion." It means, "to rule, reign, exercise power over events, actions and circumstances."

The word "DEO" (Matthew 18:18) is the Greek word for "binding" which means "legally bound, binding, or bound." We have legal rights to exercise authority over the weapon of binding and losing.

The Hebrew word "HA-SATAN" (Zechariah 3:2) indicates, "accuser, opponent, enemy, a hater, or an adversary." Anyone who prevents you, unlawfully, from successfully arriving at your destination using all foul means to bring destruction, delay or pain is an agent of Satan.

Now that we know some of these key meanings, we can now ask the question, "What is my right and authority to counteract these things?"

We cannot initiate self-deliverance without knowledge and revelation from the Word of God; we must learn to bind and loose (Matthew 16:16, Matthew 18:19). The spiritual life of the individual far outweighs any physical situation. When we learn the art of conquering in the spiritual realm, physical circumstances are controllable and manageable.

We need freedom to discharge, to liberate and to undo the heavy chains, and break free from self. We need self-deliverance. When we acquire this knowledge, we will have the power over sin and sickness, and Satan will be powerless towards us (Luke 13:12 NKJV).

We can only liberate self from the shackles of darkness through the right knowledge of the Word of God and revelation on how to defeat Satan and his forces (Ephesians 6:12).

Chapter Two:
Understanding Self

The definition of deliverance: "1. The act of delivering or the condition of being delivered. 2. Rescue from bondage or danger. 3. A publicly expressed opinion or judgment, such as the verdict of a jury."

Many people do not acknowledge that they are serving a life imprisonment of self-destruction and would rather put up a show for the rest of their lives than to face the truth.

John 5: 1-11 (NKJV), "Sometime later, Jesus went up to Jerusalem for one of the Jewish festivals. Now there is in Jerusalem near the Sheep Gate a pool, which in Aramaic is called Bethesda and which is surrounded by five covered colonnades. Here a great number of disabled people used to lie — the blind, the lame, the paralyzed. One who was there had been an invalid for thirty-eight years. When Jesus saw him lying there and learned that he had been in this condition for a long time, he asked him, "Do you want to get well?"

"Sir," the invalid replied, "I have no one to help me into the pool when the water is stirred. While I am trying to get in, someone

else goes down ahead of me."

Then Jesus said to him, "Get up! Pick up your mat and walk." At once, the man was cured; he picked up his mat and walked.

The day on which this took place was a Sabbath, and so the Jewish leaders said to the man who had been healed, "It is the Sabbath; the law forbids you to carry your mat."

But he replied, "The man who made me well said to me, 'Pick up your mat and walk.'"

This man at the well of Bethsaida had lived the life of a convict of self for 38 years. He looked to man to deliver him and year after year the help never came until the Great Deliverer, the Lion of the Tribe of Judah, the Almighty God, showed up. He did not know himself well enough to understand that man is limited and cannot be depended on.

He lost sight of who he was and focused on his lameness which seemed to define him. This condition had blinded his inner man and made him lose sight of who he was in the eyes of his Creator. He looked to a "man" who would be his salvation instead of the Savior Himself. He was not alone; many of us see ourselves in need of a helping hand and have been looking to man, instead of the One Who made us.

Are you looking to people for deliverance, to take you

from the jail of self to freedom? Are you looking to man for help in finances, joy, and peace? As long as your eyes are focused on man, the Deliverer and the jail breaker will not pass by your jail house.

From the beginning of the world, the destruction of the human race has been self. Adam and Eve had everything going well for them; but when they exercised their will, they brought on themselves destruction. What was once a promising future was turned into a life of pain and hardship.

Why would people with everything going well for them risk it all? Every problem the human race has is rooted in the wrong choice.

We are the sum total of the choices we make; the series of the choices we make define who we become. From an early age, we have made a choice of good or bad, easy or hard, effort or laziness, obedience or disobedience. In every turn, the choices we make push us along to the life we find ourselves in.

Based on some of these choices, who are we? Remember there is what God intended us to be, and what we become based on our choices. Every created thing derives its identity from the Creator. Every product in the market bears the label of the manufacturer based on what it was intended to accomplish.

Our view of what we are is faulty. It is not God's mistake, but our failure to live according to the manufacturer's manual.

To understand self, we have to look at what the Creator created – the functionality of the creation.

Genesis 1:26-27 (NKJV), Then God said, "Let Us make man in Our image, according to Our likeness; let them have dominion over the fish of the sea, over the birds of the air, and over the cattle, over all the earth and over every creeping thing that creeps on the earth." So God created man in His own image; in the image of God He created him; male and female He created them."

First, we were created to share in the image of God, to be like God in nature and character and to possess the power to rule over the creation.

The question is this: do you feel like you share in the image of God? Do you live as though you actually possess a share of God's nature and character in your life? Are you ruling or are you being dominated by creation, situations and circumstances?

If you do not know that you are what God described as His creation, keep reading and we will correct this faulty view.

We are our worst critics and most people look to others to compliment them and build them up. In many cases, these people end up tearing others down with their words knowingly or unwillingly sending many to their self-closet, and only the power of the Almighty God can bring deliverance to them.

God created you with a manual from heaven declaring that you were created in the likeness of God. Nothing is missing to empower you to accomplish what you are meant to fulfill, according to the divine purpose for which God created you.

Ruth 2:22-23 (NKJV), "Naomi said to Ruth her daughter-in-law, "It will be good for you, my daughter, to go with the women who work for him, because in someone else's field you might be harmed."

So Ruth stayed close to the women of Boaz to glean until the barley and wheat harvests were finished. And she lived with her mother-in-law.

Ruth was a foreigner who had every disadvantage stacked against her: she had lost her husband and her father in law, and had to relocate and start afresh. She did not consider how she would be treated as a foreigner who did not worship the same God. Instead, she followed every instruction of her mother in law without looking at the odds against her or feeling inferior in this foreign land.

Her strength and perception lead her to become the wife of a great rich man. Had she been fearful of self or status, and perceived herself as a widow with no helper, she would have lived a downtrodden life. Do you feel like you have everything against you? There is hope, but you must exchange the mirror with which you currently view yourself for the eyes of God Who created you.

Maybe negative and painful words were hurled at you by someone whose opinion was very valuable to you. Maybe a parent said, "You are stupid and you will never go very far." Maybe it was a spouse who said, "You are ugly and no one will want you." Perhaps a teacher or preacher said, "You don't have what it takes to be successful." This devastated you and no matter how you have tried to forget it and move on it has stuck on your rear-view mirror. Perhaps this made you lose hope in yourself and believe that you could never amount to anything good. Those words may have hurt you too deeply and made your spirit and soul walk hunched over in dismay; you agreed with those words because you had not read the last chapter of your destiny written by your Creator Himself.

"Joseph had a dream, and when he told it to his brothers, they hated him all the more. He said to them, "Listen to this dream I had: We were binding sheaves of grain out in the field when suddenly my sheaf rose and stood upright, while your sheaves gathered around mine and bowed down to it."

His brothers said to him, "Do you intend to reign over us? Will you actually rule us?" And they hated him all the more because of his dream and what he had said." (Genesis

37:5 NKJV)

Joseph encountered harsh treatment; He expected encouragement, but he found jealousy and harsh words that made him retreat and keep to himself. The very words his brothers had used to despise him came to haunt them many years later; when they had to literally fall on their knees before him, in fear.

"So Judah and his brothers came to Joseph's house, and he was still there; and they fell before him on the ground." (Gen. 44:14)

This treatment could have sent Joseph into depression while he was in jail in Egypt, causing him to lose hope in the God Who had given him the dreams to begin with. However, he held on to those dreams knowing the God of his forefathers did not lie.

Maybe God has spoken over you, yet the outside circumstances do not seem to confirm what your inside knows. It has been a long time since God sent His Word for you and you seem to be heading in the wrong direction of your promise. Hang in there, keep your faith and hope in God. Joseph was there too. He knew from the promise of his dream that God would make him great, yet he was thrown in a hole, sold as a slave, and then in jail. That seemed to be the very opposite direction of the fulfillment of his dreams; everything that surrounded him spoke of a miserable life ahead.

The jail sentence he was serving gave him new titles: a man of dubious character, a criminal record holder and a jail bird. Did he have reason to hope? None, if you are reading from the chapter of his life, "Joseph the jail bird" or "Joseph, a meal for wild animals"; but God turned all his chains, all the accusations, all the insults, pain, and disappointment into joy and victory that eventually saved a whole generation, including the Jewish nation.

His hope in God kept him alive and grounded during the toughest times of his life, when he was alone and in a strange country.

This may be a photocopy of your life, and you feel the well of hope inside you has no more water to bring forth. You just want to give up because you feel it's easier than to fight. This comes out in every step you take. You have condemned yourself and sentenced yourself to life imprisonment, but God still has a divine purpose for your life, and a divine plan to release you into your destiny.

"As he neared Damascus on his journey, suddenly a light from heaven flashed around him. He fell to the ground and heard a voice say to him, "Saul, Saul, why do you persecute me?" (Acts 9:4)

"Who are you, Lord?" Saul asked. "I am Jesus, whom you are persecuting," he replied. "Now get up and go into the city, and you will be told what you must do."

(Acts 9:5)

Paul had the rap sheet of offences of a murderer, a hater, and persecutor of the Christians. When he encountered Jesus on his way to Damascus, his life changed. He was consumed with passion in his quest to destroy the Christians. He was the chief campaigner of the destroyer which eroded his self-worth and left him an empty shell, in need of a savior.

If Jesus could salvage Saul, a man with blood of the saints of God on his hands, can he not save you in the mess you are in? Paul had scales in his eyes; he needed deliverance to allow him to see not only what damage he had caused the people of God, but also the purpose for which he was created. And look at how much God inspired Paul to accomplish for His glory, and for mankind. Look at the churches he founded, the number of Books in the New Testament the Holy Spirit led him to write, the lives he impacted.

Look up, the Author and Finisher of your life is not done with you yet. You need deliverance of self to bring you to the same page of your Author, the Lord Jesus.

You must turn away your rear-view mirror where the mistakes of yesterday may still be encrypted. Turn the stream that flows from Emmanuel's veins and let it wash away those mistakes. His precious blood leaves no marks, it wipes clean and a new slate emerges.

"Listen, 'And the blood of Jesus His Son cleanses us from all sin." 1 John 1:7 (NASB)

Chapter Three:
Self Destruction

"Now the works of the flesh are evident, which are: adultery, fornication, uncleanness, lewdness, idolatry, sorcery, hatred, contentions, jealousies, outbursts of wrath, selfish ambitions, dissensions, heresies, envy, murders, drunkenness, revelries, and the like; of which I tell you beforehand, just as I also told you in time past, that those who practice such things will not inherit the kingdom of God." (Galatians 5:19-21 NASB)

Self-destruction is the result of the works of the flesh. When we engage in adultery, we cater to the flesh without regard of the pain we will inflict on our loved ones.

We put on the line, the lives of our children who will experience the dysfunction of our broken and strained relationship with our spouses. More than that, we bind ourselves with spiritual bondages that can take us into spiral wretchedness in our lives.

Each one of these works of the flesh is an evil spirit looking for a home. Once it settles in, it begins to cater to the will of Satan, which is killing, stealing and destroying everything that is good in your life.

These things are the devil's trap to bind you so you do not inherit the Kingdom of God. Let me show you what you are missing from the Kingdom of God when you engage in these things.

"... righteousness and peace and joy in the Holy Spirit." (Roman 14:17b NKJV)

We miss our right standing before God (any time we approach God), and the devil can now petition for God not to hear us. And because God is a just God, He will be obligated to honor Satan's request, and not our request.

We also forfeit God's peace. Jesus said, *"Peace I leave with you, My peace I give to you; not as the world gives do I give to you. Let not your heart be troubled, neither let it be afraid." (John 14:27 NASB)*

I don't know about you, but life is sweet when you have peace. The peace of the world is hinged on the world of material wealth; God-peace is hinged on God, Who is able to do exceedingly and abundantly more than what we can ask, think, imagine or pray for. The world's materials change and are not adequate to meet all our needs. There are millionaires lying in hospitals, and the wealth cannot help. There are millionaires hooked on drugs, for they have no peace.

But those who have God's peace enjoy life; like Apostle Paul said, *"Not that I speak in regard*

16

to need, for I have learned in whatever state I am, to be content: I know how to be abased, and I know how to abound. Everywhere and in all things I have learned both to be full and to be hungry, both to abound and to suffer need. I can do all things through Christ who strengthens me." (Philippians 4:11-13 NKJV)

The company you keep can also be a contributing factor of the road you are on for self-destruction. The Bible says, *"Do not be misled: Bad company corrupts good character." (1 Corinthians 15:33 NJKV)*

You may be of a good character but you are keeping company with people of questionable character; this can change who you are and bring you on the road to self-destruction.

You may feel the need to fit in with this company of friends, and to be one of them, you may find yourself comprising the values you once held dear. Before you know it, you are doing exactly what they do. You may look in the mirror and not recognize the person you see in the reflection.

You may know you need deliverance, but are unable to wake yourself up from the bondage that seems to bind you. You may give up and resign to a life of self-destruction.

The good news is that the Word of God says, *"The thief comes only to steal and kill and destroy;*

I have come that they may have life, but have it to the full." (John 10:10 NKJV) The plan of the devil is that you have a miserable life, and lose your eternal life. On the other hand, Jesus came so that you may not live in a life of self-destruction, self-hatred, or a defeated life, but "have it to the full."

God had His eyes focused on you before you were even conceived in your mother's womb. He had a plan set out to bless you and He sent His best, His son Jesus, that you may have a life you can enjoy and live to the fullest, aided by the Holy Spirit.

The comfort of the company you keep may be hard to leave; you may feel like you will be lost in a web of loneliness, but in the arena where people of destiny operate it is populated by a small number of people. The arena of people who walk with no purpose is crowded. The saying "misery loves company" is very true. You will find great company and short term friendship in the arena where misery lives. Destiny destroyers or delayers are many and that is the work of the devil – to steal your dreams, hopes and purpose.

His primary purpose is to kill the man God created in the image and likeness of Himself and leave behind a shadow of the original man, who lives from day to day with no hope or joy.

"So God created mankind in his own image, in the image of God he created them, So God created mankind in his own image, in the

image of God he created them." (Genesis 1:27 19 NKJV)

He will eventually destroy you and lead you to hell if you don't receive deliverance and a change of heart, mind and soul.

You can move out of this company; not on your own, but through deliverance and keeping the company of Christ seekers who are working on the God-written chapters of their destinies as well.
You are not alone in this walk. Christ's saving blood is still available and can wash away all sins, break every bondage and set you free to walk in the fullness of your calling in Christ Jesus.

"For God so loved the world that he gave his one and only Son, that whoever believes in him shall not perish but have eternal life." (John 3:16 NKJV)

This verse amplifies the desire and love of God for you, that God gave His ultimate possession, His Son Jesus. It cost God His only begotten Son, so that you may live in joy, hope, strength, purposefully, and at the end of this earthly chapter, you may continue your journey of eternal life. The song writer put it in the right perspective, "Just for me, just for me, Jesus came and did it, just for me".

When Christ was on the Cross, your sins were on His mind and in His entire body; and when He said *"It is finished" (John 19:30 NKJV)*, you were part of the people whose sins were taken away that day. You, therefore, have no reason to sentence yourself to life of imprisonment when Jesus took the sentence for you.

The reality of the matter is that your mistakes were paid for even before you were born. Therefore, you only need to accept the "jail free" card and walk out of the jailhouse center into a life of freedom.

Chapter Four:
The War Within

"I say then: Walk in the Spirit, and you shall not fulfill the lust of the flesh. For the flesh lusts against the Spirit, and the Spirit against the flesh; and these are contrary to one another, so that you do not do the things that you wish. But if you are led by the Spirit, you are not under the law." (Galatians 5:16-18 NKJV) If what we have read so far is true, how comes we still struggle to do what is right? How comes I am still in bondage?

Apostle Paul opened our minds to see the conflict of the battle within. This battle within each one of us is between our flesh, which has dominated our lives, and our spirit, which tries to connect with God's Spirit; for we are spirit, soul and also a body (flesh). Remember, everything that we learn is through our five physical senses.

Someone once said that the greatest battle is the one between the ears, i.e. the head or the mind. The raging battle in our mind is fighting against that which we perceive as right. Sometimes, we really want to do that right thing: wake up and read our Bible, leave that draining relationship, develop a clean language that glorifies God. Even though you know what you

21

should do, the ability or discipline to do it fails you.

Mark 14:38, "Watch and pray so that you will not fall into temptation. The spirit is willing, but the flesh is weak." The will of the flesh or man takes over and you end up doing what you don't want to do.

Every New Year Day, many people of every walk of life speak of resolutions for the New Year. They vow to follow these resolutions to better their lives, one way or the other. Gyms all over the world experience a surge in enrollment at the beginning of each year. The gyms are forced to employ more trainers to cope with the sudden surge that comes with the New Year resolutions.

The right intentions are there, the hopes and dreams are there, but just a few weeks later, the number of the gym goers dwindles as members lose the fight with their resolution. Do these gym members have a weight problem? Yes, they do. Do they desperately want to get into shape? Yes, they do. So what is the missing ingredient in this equation? The battle they are trying to fight is still raging in their minds. They must win the mind battle.

Some people resolve to go to church every Sunday without fail. They attend the midweek services and support their church as much as they can. They faithfully attend church in January, but come February, they start losing the battle.

They truly want to serve God but they lose the battle and give in to the excuses that the mind relates to the body. In order to win this war, the mind has to win first and then the body will follow. Yes, you can win it. Jesus knew this and He said, "...**With man this is impossible, but not with God; all things are possible with God.**" (Mark 10:27 NKJV)

There are many cases where women remain in abusive relationships and endure great physical and mental abuse. The perpetrator could be a boyfriend or a husband, someone who is supposed to be their protector. The perpetrator abuses them and then loves them in that same breath, all the while giving them all kinds of excuses for their abusive conduct.

Her physical form knows this is wrong and she should run but her mind battles saying the boyfriend or husband love her and therefore, she must have been the cause of the abuse.

The only way this lady is able to get out of this situation is to win the battle from within, so as to tackle the physical one. The mind has to win this battle that you are in, and for you to know that you are better than this. It has been done and can be done.

The battle from within has hindered many from achieving many great achievements; the fear of failing, the belief that you cannot achieve much, according to your parents, friends, spouse, etc.

You may need deliverance from that self-defeat spirit

so that you can embrace the power that God has put in you and bring to life what the Bible says of you... *"I can do all this through him who gives me strength." (Philippians 4:13 NKJV)*

The war within you is more deadly than the battles fought by soldiers on the war frontlines. The enemy is fighting a losing war. However no one can help you unless you surrender completely to the loving presence and power of God. It is He and He alone Who can bless you with the deliverance you need.

Chapter Five:
Win the War

I pray that by now you have identified the wars that are going on; that you understand that Christ has won the victory. Christ's victory has to be applied to your battles. This is the only way in which you will be set free.

Let us examine a woman from the Bible who battled with her thoughts and emotions; she was ostracized by her community and loved ones; and she was terribly afflicted by a severe illness in her body. She fought all of this, and she won.

"And a woman having an issue of blood twelve years, which had spent all her living upon physicians, neither could be healed of any, Came behind him, and touched the border of his garment: and immediately her issue of blood stanched.

And Jesus said, Who touched me? When all denied, Peter and they that were with him said, Master, the multitude throng thee and press thee, and sayest thou, Who touched me?

And Jesus said, Somebody hath touched me:

for I perceive that virtue is gone out of me.

And when the woman saw that she was not hid, she came trembling, and falling down before him, she declared unto him before all the people for what cause she had touched him, and how she was healed immediately."
(Luke 8:43-48 NKJV)

She was rejected by society because of the battle she was facing in her physical body and in her mind. No one wanted to sit or be associated with her. You can imagine the mental anguish she was feeling: no friend, no family or even society to support her during the worst chapter of her life. She tried all she could by going to all the medical specialists she could find for a cure, so that she would be accepted back in the society. Perhaps you are in the same position, trying to do what would make you loved or feel complete by family and friends but it has not yielded much.

This woman with the issue of blood used all of her resources, and perhaps borrowed and sold her properties, to get healed. This was not an ordinary illness; in those days, any illness like the one she had required one to live away from "normal" people. Are you living in isolation in your mind? Do you feel you have made too many mistakes? Or it may be that you are living in a sinful life and you are not sure how to stop and make a U-turn.

God availed this book for you that you may walk free from the mind jail you currently find yourself in. When this woman had lost all hope, money, friends, and family she heard of a man. She must have heard in passing as she was not allowed to be in the company of others according to the culture. She heard of a man named Jesus, Who was healing men, women and children. She even heard that He was raising the dead. Can you imagine how a tiny flicker of hope began to light up in her? Then she listened closely and heard He was actually passing by her city. She took mental details and she started plotting day and night how she could reach and touch this man, Jesus. Are you looking for a deliverer, who can take away your sickness and stop you from heading in the wrong direction?

There is a man named Jesus.

She must have figured which back route she would take as she could not take the road everyone else took. She may have hid in the bushes afraid of being seen and waited.

When the noisy crowd started approaching where she hid, she may have heard people calling the name of Jesus and begging to be healed. And when Jesus stopped to minister to someone, she crawled under everyone's feet and grabbed on Jesus' garment as that was the closest she could get.

Instantly she got her healing. Her mind battles ceased and the freedom of the healing of her body flowed. The shame left, the hopelessness left and the blood flow stopped.

Her world stood still.

Perhaps you are like this woman. You may have read, the "positive thinking" books, watched videos on steps to "be happy again", but the battle in your mind still rages. The Lord Jesus is the only one who can do a complete overhaul of the mind, body and soul. Healing of the mind and body of this woman brought confidence and strength to her. She was no longer an outcast in her community. She became just as whole as anyone else.

"And Jesus said, Who touched me? When all denied, Peter and they that were with him said, Master, the multitude throng thee and press thee, and sayest thou, Who touched me?" (Luke 8:45 NKJV)

She lost the shame, and acknowledged she had touched Him; she told Him she had been sick but was now healed by extending her faith and touching the hem of the clothing Jesus wore. Are you desperate enough to do whatever it takes to receive healing of your body, mind and soul?

Jehovah "Rapha", the healer, is here, and He heals and does "restorative surgery" from head to toe. The battles in your mind and in your soul were settled at Calvary more than 2000 years ago. But you must apply that redemptive victory that was won for you by Jesus on the Cross. Isaiah 53:5 says, *"But he was pierced for our rebellion, crushed for our sins. He was beaten so we could be whole.*

He was whipped so we could be healed." The price has already been paid. He took our rebellion, our sin and He paid with his life, and healing became yours from that moment. Healing of mind, body and soul was paid for at the highest price, which is the very life and precious blood of Jesus.

A story is told of a man whose parents died and during the reading of the will, he realized to his dismay that his mother left a Bible for him.

More than likely, he was looking forward to real estate and loads of money but none came.

In utter disappointment he walked away, threw the Bible on the book shelf and angrily grumbled under his breath. He did not live a Christian life and suffered lack and he struggled for many years.

In utter desperation, he decided to seek God, went to the book shelf and dusted off the Bible which, by now, had accumulated a lot of dust. He flipped and began to read and he realized he was living a life that was not pleasing to God. He began to see the goodness of the Lord and His mercies and gradually let the bitterness and anger he felt for so many years against his mother fade.

As he flipped the pages, something fell out and he bent to pick it up. It was a note detailing where all the properties and riches of his parents were. You can imagine his shock.

All this time he was living a life short of what his parents intended for him in their will. He had an inheritance with his name on it and all he had needed was to obey the instructions to access it.

That may be you right now. You could be living in a battle field, wounded and bleeding while that battle had been won many years ago on Calvary's Cross. You will keep fighting and dealing with fiery darts of the enemy on your mind and body until you come to the reading of the will which Jesus left for you, detailing all you have through faith in Him.

I could give you a check for a million dollars today, write your name on it and sign it and you could remain poor for the rest of your life, even though the check is sitting on your table. You must follow the process set up by the bank. You must take that check to the bank and have it processed and funds banked into your account.

The same applies in the spiritual world. You must follow the procedure and steps to get your deliverance, healing and full restoration, through personal faith in Jesus.

You must apply the instructions which enable you to reap the full benefits of being a child of God and being a victor in this walk of life.

The story of the prodigal son brings home this point of realizing you are heading in the wrong direction and you need to make a U-Turn to start on the journey to victory.

"After he had spent everything, there was a severe famine in that whole country, and he began to be in need. So he hired himself out to a citizen of that country, who sent him to his fields to feed pigs. He longed to fill his stomach with the pods that the pigs were eating, but no one gave him anything.

"When he came to his senses, he said, 'How many of my father's hired servants have food to spare, and here I am starving to death! I will set out and go back to my father and say to him: Father, I have sinned against heaven and against you. I am no longer worthy to be called your son; make me like one of your hired servants.' So he got up and went to his father.

"But while he was still a long way off, his father saw him and was filled with compassion for him; he ran to his son, threw his arms around him and kissed him.

"The son said to him, 'Father, I have sinned against heaven and against you. I am no longer worthy to be called your son.'

"But the father said to his servants, 'Quick! Bring the best robe and put it on him. Put a ring on his finger and sandals on his feet. (Luke 15:14-22 NKJV)

This prodigal son squandered his inheritance and he began living worse than any servant who was employed by his father. Things got so bad that he ate with pigs, which was the lowest level he could have reached. His father was a rich influential man and this son had everything going for him till he made a decision to step out of his father's protection.

We also fight battles because of disobedience and when we have been wounded and completely desperate, then we call on God for a rescue. The father in this story is a replica of our Father in heaven, plenteous in mercy and loving. He waits day and night when we can call on Him for mercy and deliverance.

So today, you have come to the right place, realizing that in our Father's house there are blessings and healing and you can be whole again.

The Bible states the most important words in this text, "when he came to his senses", meaning he came to his end of the road sign and suddenly it dawned on him that he didn't need to live his life in misery.

To win this war within is very important, and it's won by acknowledging that you cannot do it on your own and that you are in you need of a deliverer. That will cause you to overcome and have the victory.

The prodigal son won the battle physically and mentally, and he said" I will go to my father..." He put aside the shame of what people would say; what his family would think of him; and even how he felt inside or looked outside.

He had an 'aha!' moment; the light inside suddenly went on. He knew he had to do whatever he needed to do to get to his father's house. He knew once he got to his father's house all his hunger, disappointment and mistakes will be taken care of.

Jesus of Nazareth, the Great Deliverer will deliver and heal you, and restore your mind, body and soul.

Welcome to the deliverance of your body, mind and soul.

Chapter Six:
Spiritual Discerment

The discerning of spirits is the ability to identify the kind of spirit that is the driving force behind a particular condition, event or person. Spiritual discernment is the grace to see into the unseen. It is a gift of the Spirit that enables you to perceive what is in the spirit. Its purpose is to see into the nature of what is hidden and be able to know how to deal with it.

Without discernment, one will not be able to understand what is going on around them. You need a spiritual eye to judge circumstances and events. There are three kinds of spirits in operation around us all. The first are heavenly spirits, the second are evil spirits and the last are human spirits. The heavenly spirits include angels and the Spirit of God.

These forces will either be a blessing or a hindrance to one's promotion in life. Without proper insight, one will be caught up in a web of chaos and deceit. This breeds delay, frustration and pain in one's life. It is always important to understand the environment one is in. You must be able to dominate it to bring success and happiness.

The Bible says, *"I get understanding therefore*

I had every false way. Your word is a lamp onto my feet, and a light onto my path."
(Psalm 119: 104-105 NKJV)

We need to illuminate the path that God has set for us so that we do not slip and hurt ourselves. God is the true source of discernment. He highlights our path to understand spiritual darkness that is operating around us. One needs to hear the voice of God concerning spiritual matters that have an effect on the physical realm. The key to hearing God's voice is meditation on the Word of God and prayer, a two-way communication. The second key is building a personal, intimate relationship with God. Thirdly, one must perceive the voice of God through the different means that God will place before you. These then become a yardstick and a spiritual compass to direct your path.

The Holy Spirit prompts you to perceive God's voice; God may speak to you through spiritual dreams, visions, visitations, prophetic words or a conversation with a friend that brings revelation.

In this way, Heaven has opened over you through an avenue of God's creation. Your responsibility is to know that God is speaking to you. You must align yourself with the instructions that are coming from His voice. Most of the time your spirit will register the uncommon nature of the communication that you are receiving in your spirit.

Your mind may try to seek or create confusion and

tell you that the voice you are hearing is not God's, but self. God is always precise and accurate. His timing is always impeccable. He will speak to you in a manner that accords with the Bible.

While discerning spirits, you will be caught up within different images, pictures and scenarios which may contain instructions or directions to your promise land. Sometimes, God will send your Moses to deliver and direct you from your Egypt to your Canaan. Should you refuse to listen to your inner voice, you will end up making grave mistakes that can be very expensive. These mistakes may delay your growth and your success of arriving at your destination.

Discernment is an instrument that is created by God for man's direction in the ways of God. Observance and knowing the inner voice that is bringing peace and direction to your circumstances will result in a positive end result; this will show you that God is speaking to you.

Pictures and images may appear to you in your mind, dreams or through a vision. This could either be God or Satan speaking to you. However, God-centered discernment will always be for your promotion and multiplication. The more you seek God's face and walk with Him, the sharper your discernment becomes. Therefore, you will be able to navigate your way in life and arrive successfully at your port of call.

Sometimes, discerning wrongly will result in a delay in your life, frustration in your plans and pain to your pathway. Lack of discernment from God and His Word or His chosen servants can cause you so much pain. Our roots and our family tree create circumstances that require discernment to know what choices to make.

When we fail to know this, we will hit a brick wall which makes life very difficult and causes us to go through continuous headaches and nightmares. This will continue for your generation, as well as the generation that follows you. Lack of godly discernment brings pain to your destiny and the generation after you. Your legacy suffers and your inheritance diminishes because of alternatives that might be placed before you.

Chapter Seven:
Choices &
Consequences

God has given each one of us a great opportunity to determine the outcome of our destiny. Inbuilt in these choices are two great results: a reward of success or a future of pain.

In Obadiah 1:17 it reads, *"But on Mount Zion there shall be deliverance, and there shall be holiness; The house of Jacob shall possess their possessions."* It is a choice that you have to take to possess your inheritance. You are always responsible for the outcome of your life though your roots, culture and environment may speak otherwise.

God has given all of us power and authority to override every scheme that does not favor us. Until we come to the realization of this, we will always be in bondage to the enemy's plans. For example, the Word reads that, *"Behold, I give you the authority to trample on serpents and scorpions, and over all the power of the enemy, and nothing shall by any means hurt you." (Luke 10:19 NKJV)* The choice is always yours to take a side with either good or bad, blessings or curses.

Your actions will attract the corresponding blessing or curse. Sometimes, our past generations inflict upon us curses, pain and struggle which follow us after birth. As we gain knowledge in God, we are able to examine our circumstances and judge whether things are going according to our favor or they are working against us.

It is because we lack knowledge of the Word of God, we end up maintaining the same status quo of curse, failure and struggle that our ancestors held; and we cry out without receiving any help.

God's intent is to bless us, it has always been this way. The Word reads: ***"then the Lord knows how to deliver the godly out of temptations and to reserve the unjust under punishment for the day of judgment," (2 Peter 2:9 NKJV).*** From this verse we can see that it is God's heart to see us succeed. He wants to bring you to your promise land! He does not force anyone against their own will, however, He gives you your freedom of choice as well as your will with which you make and take the reward or consequence of said choice.

"I call heaven and earth as witnesses today against you, that I have set before you life and death, blessing and cursing; therefore choose life, that both you and your descendants may live;" (Deuteronomy 30:19 NKJV).

When we begin to think that God is far away from us, and will not be affected by our life, our choices become unbalanced. We then make great mistakes that give us agony in our present circumstances, with the overflow of those hurts being reserved for the generation that will follow us.

God has given each of us instructions to follow His Word, and His holy human servants who are present to guide us, and to deliver us from the bondage of indecision and curses that have been transferred from our roots. For example, the Word reads, ***"Stand fast therefore in the liberty by which Christ has made us free and do not be entangled again with a yoke of bondage." (Galatians 5:1 NKJV)***

The wrong choices that we make will prevent us from being delivered and from enjoying the full blessings of God. Life can be painful without guidance and leadership from those who have gone ahead of us.

To be fully delivered, one must have knowledge of God and an understanding of the consequences of our actions. We must also align ourselves with goals that will bring us success rather than hurt. Satan's job is to slow us down through decisions that are not godly or healthy for our spiritual welfare. By the time we are at the crossroads of our decision, the enemy's plan is then revealed, which is too late.

"The thief does not come except to steal, and to kill, and to destroy. I have come that they may have life, and that they may have it more abundantly." (John 10:10 NKJV)

God wants to bless you. Make a choice to run and go with God. Commit your life and the life of your family into the hands of God, as Joshua did:

"...as for me and my house, we will serve the Lord." (Joshua 24:15 NKJV)

It is through this way that the glory of God will go before you. His power will defend you. His grace will sustain you. Your generation will find peace in the country that God has placed you in.

PRAYERS FOR DELIVERANCE

Prayer of Salvation

Father God, I know that I am a sinner. I accept that I have made mistakes and decisions in my life that have distanced me from You, Your Son Jesus and grieved Your Holy Spirit. I am truly sorry for these things, and I acknowledge my sin in going against Your will and way. Have mercy on me. Forgive me of all my sins.

Lead me as I embark on this new journey of salvation. Jesus, I invite You into my heart right this moment. I accept You, Jesus, as my personal Lord and Saviour. I ask You, Holy Spirit, to fill me, cleanse me of all my sins and correct me as I go about my life.

Heavenly Father, I re-dedicate my life to you. I offer myself as a living sacrifice. Take my hands and let them be used to do Your will. Take my legs and let them be used to walk in the way of righteousness. Take my life and let it sing Your praises. Take my mind and let it think on those things that are true, pure, kind and godly. Take my heart and let it meditate on Your Word, love others as You have loved me and seek after You continuously.

I thank You, Father, for Your salvation! I thank You that You have cleansed me of all unrighteousness and have made me a part of Your eternal family. I thank You for Your love, I thank You for Your peace and protection.

Help me, Heavenly Father, to walk on the right path as I embark on this journey of faith and deliverance. Thank you for Your protection and guidance in advance. I pray in the name of Jesus. Amen.

Breaking Family Curses

Father God, I give You thanks and glory that through the knowledge of Your Word no weapon formed against me shall prosper; and every tongue that rises itself against me in judgement, I condemn it (Isaiah 54:17).

Every family tree that is not planted by You, Oh God, concerning my destiny, today, I declare it dead in the name of Jesus. I command the roots to be stifled of life; my freedom to go forward is established.

I speak to every curse that I have inherited, knowingly or unknowingly, by virtue of my connection with my ancestors from time past. I denounce the operation and abolish the activities of these curses that have followed me till now, and command their demise in the name of Jesus.

I declare that their institutions and cultural activities surrounding my birth are abolished. I am free to go forward joyfully and full of hope from now. I possess my inheritance. I declare that I am delivered from the powers of darkness and translated into the Kingdom of God's dear Son, Christ Jesus (Colossians 1:13).

I take the shield of faith and quench every fiery dart of all generational curses that had prevailed against me. I speak to every work of darkness that I have inherited as a result of my bloodline, and I bind you, in the name of Jesus. You will no longer have an adverse effect on me. Today, I declare my independence of generational curses from birth, in the name of Jesus. I pray this in the name of Jesus. Amen.

Family Repentance

Father God, I repent of every generational curse that my forefathers inherited. I declare that I am no longer a partaker of the pain of that curse today. I ask You, in the name of Jesus, that my offspring and posterity and I be washed with the blood of Jesus. Set me free to go forward and inherit my blessings. I cut every link of curses, pain and shame that has come upon my life due to my connection with my former life.

I repent of all sins I have committed in any form or shape, and any activities that I engaged in during my former days, that are currently making me suffer. I announce, in the name of Jesus, that I am free, for the Bible says in John 8:36 that if the Son makes you free, you shall be free indeed.

I repent on behalf of my father and mother, of whom I am a product. Every curse that they inherited, through which I am now suffering, I denounce them in the name of Jesus. I declare that I am the righteousness of God in Christ Jesus (2 Corinthians 5:21).

I declare that from today, no curse of my former days or in my family lineage has any effect on my life. My present picture of disaster and failure fade away into the blood of Jesus. I walk into the fullness of the blessings of God for the Lord has forgiven me of my sins and delivered me from all unrighteousness.

I pray in the name of Jesus. Amen.

Self-Repentance

Heavenly Father, I repent of my own sins that I have committed that have resulted in my current circumstances. I bring myself under the shadow of the Almighty God. My former life of disobedience, which has cost me so much pain, I now denounce in the name of Jesus.

Every careless relationship and all sinful activities I have initiated that have brought me into darkness and sadness, I reject that spirit now in the name of Jesus. My spirit is free, my soul is healed and my body is revived! I embrace the full power of the Almighty God through my personal faith in Jesus, my Lord and Saviour.

I claim the glory of God to flow over my life as water pours over a mountain ridge. I am blessed to take possession of my blessings and to run the race of success. I praise you Lord that today, during my deliverance by Your grace and mercy, I declare that you, oh Lord, are my rock, my fortress, and my deliverance (2 Samuel 22:2).

I thank You, Father, that I am finally delivered from the strong enemy and from them that hate me; for they are no longer too strong for me. For You, oh Lord, have brought me forth into a large place and You have delivered me because You delight in me and have made me what I am now (2 Samuel 22:20). I thank You, Father God, that You have brought me forth from my enemies and have also lifted me up on high, above those that rose up against me; for You, Oh Lord, have delivered me from violent people. I am FREE! I pray in the name of Jesus. Amen.

Breaking the Spirit of Control

Father God, I bless Your great and mighty name. By Your goodness and mercy, You have released me from the fallow ground and hardened areas of my life. By Your goodness, You have set me free to walk onto my higher ground. I break forces in the air that have been responsible for all negative habits and lifestyles that have wrestled with me, in the name of Jesus (Jeremiah 4:3).

I renounce unploughed grounds in my life and any hardened habits that control my life. I declare that the price of greatness has emerged and my life has experienced the sound of the trumpet of victory. I declare that I take by force my fallow ground and translate it into a fertile ground with the power of the Holy Spirit flowing through my life, through my environment and within me.

I break all influences within and without my habitation that are moving against the will of God. I declare them broken. Every fight and battle contesting against my destiny, I denounce you and overcome you, in the name of Jesus. For I am born of God and I overcome my world! Victory is mine, in the name of Jesus (1 John 5:4).

I cast off every spirit of frustration and delay that follow me wherever I go and through whatever I do.

I declare that from now I shall experience the signs and the wonders of God following me. I am a winner and a conqueror through Christ Jesus who has ordained me to walk in victory and championship. My spirit, soul and body are free now! I thank You Lord, in the name of Jesus. Amen.

Breaking the Transfer of Family Curses

Heavenly Father, to every unclean spirit and struggles that have occurred and brought me into a dry place seeking rest, I declare You will find no more. Through the blood of Jesus, I declare my independence and innocence. The spirit of oppression, delays and chaos is officially broken by my announcement.

Every family tree which has given birth to a fruit of which I have been apart, today I denounce your activities and operation in my life. I put on the new image of Christ Jesus and I have a new glory and praise over my life. I thank You, Father, for putting Your blessings and grace over me.

I now inherit the blessings of the elected one (Colossians 3:10-12). I purge myself and accept the responsibility to walk in righteousness, knowing that I am born in Christ and worthy of His favor. The wicked spirits of my roots will no longer operate through or in me. I purge myself and am considered a vessel of honour through Christ Jesus (2 Timothy 2:21).

I walk in righteousness and the grace of God overcomes my yesterday and brings me into His marvelous light. I am more knowledgeable now to walk in the blessings and the favor of God as my former roots and relationships that did not bring blessing. Heavenly Father, I thank You, in the name of Jesus my Lord and Saviour. Amen.

The Law of the Spirit

Heavenly Father, I thank You for making me a new person in Christ Jesus. I am free from every sin and death. For the law of the Spirit of life in Christ Jesus has set me free to walk in my higher field. I possess the Spirit of Christ to rule and reign in this present world. The anointing to excel in faith in Christ Jesus now operates in me. I am able to understand the insight of Christ's grace to determine a free new life.

I am what I am in Christ Jesus. I thank God that there is a higher mystery of His godliness and power overflowing me, over and above iniquity in my life. God brings into my life His blessings of liberty and His Spirit of freedom. I am an overcomer and the Spirit of God has raised a standard on my behalf against every spirit of wickedness; as the Bible says in Isaiah 59:19, "I call heaven and earth as witnesses today against you, that I have set before you life and death, blessing and cursing; therefore choose life, that both you and your descendants may live;" (Isaiah 59:19).

I am delivered by the Spirit of the Lord from the negative forces of the law of sin. My usefulness and blessings have come because the Spirit of the Lord operates through me to conquer every force of darkness, the spirit of bondage and any spirit that has operated against my destiny.

I walk after the Spirit of God. I will fulfill my destiny

and rule and reign as a child of the Most High God. I am victorious for the Spirit of Christ rules though me. I am an overcomer for the precious Blood of Christ shields me. Heavenly Father, I thank You, in the name of my Lord and Saviour, Jesus Christ. Amen.

Anointing to Excel

I thank You, Father God, that Your Holy Spirit is causing me to excel. I am experiencing victory in all that I do from now. I have wisdom to get knowledge and understanding. I am excelling in what I am doing. I know that Your desire for my life, Father, is for good and not evil. Therefore, I declare that I am an overseer of the blessings of God. I am also a partaker of God's great blessings.

I thank You Father that Your holy angels of blessings are walking with me. I am experiencing an abundance of Your blessings and possessing my blessings. The Lord is bringing honey out of the rock for me this month. The Lord has opened all the good doors into my life. I possess breakthrough designed anointing in my life and I am living fully secure in Your presence and Your blessings.

I thank God that my destiny possesses the grace to trample over all anti-excellence spirits. I am enlarged by the glory of God and every architect of financial blessings is flowing through my life. I command all helpers from all angles of life to be in position to see my victory and excellence. I receive an automatic promotion from every department of life, flowing through my being.

I am anointed to excel and prosper in the work of my hands. A progress altar is fashioned before me to enjoy the blessings of God. I possess my benefits and I enjoy the blessings that cause me to be called a child of excellence. I move in the anointing that conquers only because You grant me the power to live a victorious life. I thank You, Father God, in the name of Jesus, my Lord and Saviour. Amen.

Prayer for Jobs & Business Success

Father God, Your Word says in 1 Timothy 5:18 that someone who works, is worthy of being paid for the work that they do. I ask You, Heavenly Father, that You will help me as I am looking for a job, career or business to pursue.

I thank You, Father, that You have put the right people in my way: suppliers, HR firms, CEO's, clients and customers who will assist me in making a good living from which I will be able to bring my tithes and offerings into Your storehouse, as well as provide for myself and my family, and the poor.

Father God Almighty, I thank You for the grace that You have given me in my job seeking and client seeking process. I thank You that people are favoring me for the positions and contract that I am looking for, in the name of Jesus.

Lord, I give You praise for all that You have done for me concerning my career situation. I praise You for all that You are about to do and all that You are doing to help me have a stable job, career and business.

You are the One Who turned Joseph from a prisoner into a prime minister and I know that same grace and anointing is upon my life, right now, in the name of Jesus. For all Your favours, I thank You, in the name of Jesus. Amen.

Prayer Against Destiny Killers

Dear Heavenly Father, I declare that I speak the wisdom of God as it is ordained to flow and reveal every destiny killer. I conquer them all, in the name of Jesus. My divine destiny appears in the cloud led by the holy angels of God to bring me into victory.

I am empowered by You, and I refuse to live below my divine standards. I declare that I am a winner against every destiny killer. I conquer every rage that my enemies have placed against me, in the name of Jesus. My eyes are anointed my hands and legs are anointed to work within my divine purpose.

Every power contending against my divine destiny is scattered and destroyed, in the name of Jesus. I release the spirit of excellence over me to destroy destiny persistent killers. I possess the right to stop all destiny harassers, in the name of Jesus. I command all powers of darkness assigned to destroy my destiny to be nullified, in the name of Jesus. May the heavens and the earth wrestle and demote every assignment against my life that is for my destruction, in the name of Jesus.

I possess my possession against all destiny killers (Obadiah 1:17). I declare that my enemies will not convert my destiny into rags. The Lord restores me into my original divine plan for my life. I thank You

Lord, that every destiny demoting name assigned against my name is destroyed and the Lord has enlarged my coast all around me, in the precious name of Jesus. Amen.

Abundance & Prosperity

Father God, thank You, for You are my God and my Lord.

"For the Lord is a sun and a shield over my life. The Lord will give grace and glory to me. No good thing will He withhold from me as I walk uprightly. The Lord of Hosts shall bless me even as I walk in trustworthiness with Him" (Psalm 84:11-12 NLT).

I am experiencing the resurrection power of the Lord Jesus upon the work of my hands now. I receive blessings over and above the competition of my enemies. I declare embargos on my progress to fall down and scatter. I celebrate my resurrection to walk in abundance and overflow. The mighty hand of God is upon me for good and keeps me from all failure and every evil wisdom and manipulation.

I embrace the invitation to walk in the appointment of God's goodness and mercy. The multitude of God's blessings gathers around my home. I am a spectator in the goodness of God's glory and a participator in His overflowing grace of abundance. I am anchored in celebration and the spirit of abundance overflows and outruns my destiny. Prosperity of God's goodness saturates my atmosphere.

The uncommon techniques to inherit the blessings of Abraham, Isaac and Jacob manifest in my life. I am ordained to enjoy the supernatural overflow of abundance of the anointing that is upon Jesus working through me. The earth opens up and releases her blessings in abundance over my destiny. For these blessings, Father God, I thank You in the name of Jesus. Amen.

Financial Breakthrough

I thank You Father God that you wish above all that I should prosper and be in health even as my soul prospers (3 John 1:2). I have financial freedom and liberty. The pathway to my financial happiness is initiated as I decree it as such even now. I call forth the anointing for financial breakthrough to rain and fall over my life and my environment. I walk in total headship anointing and grace. The Lord moves to cause financial blessings to flow in my life.

I break the backbone of any situation associated with struggle and financial nightmare. I refuse to swim in the ocean of financial problems in my life. I release the ultimate grace and power of the financial blessings that came upon the Israelites to come upon me. I thank you, Father God, that my destiny for financial excellence and financial freedom has been released. I embrace my financial overflow even now, in the name of Jesus.

I possess the insight to create financial blessings that will be released into my life. I am blessed beyond measure because the anointing for financial breakthrough runs and chases after me daily. May the holy angels on financial assignment be released to bring me into order and inherit my blessings. The prosperity anointing and grace flow through my life. My destiny is surrounded by the wealthy name of Jesus. Heavenly resources rush to my door. The Sword of the Spirit cancels out every satanic debt, in

Jesus name. Amen.

Deliverance from the Marital Destruction

Father, let Your Kingdom be established in every department of my marriage, in the name of Jesus. I renounce and denounce every evil spiritual marriage contract I have consciously and unconsciously entered into, and I declare them broken. I declare that all spirits of marital destruction on assignment against my marriage are released from me, in the name of Jesus.

Every spirit of anger, strife, familiar spirits and financial starvation spirits, I release myself from their works and plans, in the name of Jesus. I destroy and cancel every satanic plan against my home and every evil design fashioned against my marriage becomes cancelled and replaced with the blessings of God, in the name of Jesus.

My life is brought under the covenant blessings of the marriage between Christ and the Church. My home is covered with the Blood of Jesus. The boundaries of my land are shielded with the authority and the power of the grace of God. My marriage is free to be enjoyed by my life partner and myself, and all my children and posterity.

We are bound in love and spiritual blessings, in the name of Jesus. Every evil wedding ring and garment that I have put on which is not of God, I denounce it and roast it in the fire of God. My marriage is delivered from the hands of homewreckers, in the name of Jesus. Amen.

Safeguarding Your Home

Father God, in the name of Jesus, I declare that my home is protected under the shadow of the Almighty (Psalm 91:1). I release my home under the Holy Spirit's fire and protection. I command the foundation of my home to be built upon the Blood of Jesus and the Holy Spirit, and the Word of God, our Rock.

Every sin of idolatry is condemned and broken in my home and none of my offspring shall inherit an idolatrous spirit. I destroy and cancel their effect on my home and all those who live under my shelter, in the name of Jesus.
The spirit of lack of submission and authority is bound and declared null and void, and will not operate in my home. The spirit of love and fear of God resides in my home. Selfishness and any spirit of interference by in-laws are cancelled and abolished.

Every demonic spirit of traditions and covenants assigned against my home, I cancel them in the name of Jesus and I release the destiny of my home under the leadership of the Holy Spirit. The grace of God shall prevail in my home and cause my house to enjoy the anointing that brings celebration.

There shall be noise of excitement, grace and music of praise in my home. Every satanic marriage on assignment against my children is bound. My spouse and I shall submit ourselves under the anointing of the Holy Spirit. The grace of God shall create unity. Love and the fear of God will operate in our house, in the name of Jesus. Amen.

Career & Business

Father God, I thank You for blessing the work of my hands and I thank You for releasing Your untold blessings over the work of my hands. My hands are blessed to possess my possession, even as I walk in the capacity of Your goodness.

Through the grace of God over the work of my hands fruitfulness, abundance and increase arrive at the door of my life. I am called to dominate and control every work that I put my hands to do. I do a good job and I get a great reward, by the grace of God.

I attract contracts, favors, and abundance of jobs that bring me an untold financial blessing; this allows me to live above average. Because of the blessings of God over the work of my hands, I am called the blessed of the Lord. My home celebrates the fruitfulness of the glory of God.

I can do all things because my hands are blessed with the oil of gladness. I receive rewards from the Kingdom of God. I walk in higher places and in the corridors of powers where negotiations and business deals and contracts are initiated.

God has made me a good negotiator to acquire wealth and masses of supernatural blessings which make my hands possess my financial breakthrough. I am favored to possess my possessions in all endeavours of my business and career path, through the favour of God. Thank You, Lord God, in the name of Jesus. Amen.

Children

Thank You Heavenly Father, that my children are the fruits of God's grace and mercy. Every one of my children shall be called the blessed of the Lord. Each and every one of them will operate under the ultimate blessings of God, guided by the Holy Spirit.

My children are door openers at the palace of the Almighty God. They will enjoy the supernatural favor that was on Jesus and they will be counted as sons and daughters of the Most High God.

My children shall possess the gates of their enemies and their blessings will be considered the best in the completion of life. I declare my children as instruments of blessing and multiplication.

My children shall walk in the corridors of influence in this life. Their generation shall be like the stars of Heaven and the sand on the seashore. God's mighty hand shall surround them everywhere they go and His goodness and mercy shall pull them from the valley of the shadow of death.

The goodness of God covers them and surrounds them to win in every competition of this life. The generation I am watching shall be the fruit of the vine in my garden. I command the fresh rain of God and the oil of gladness to be upon them; for God considers them instruments of peace and they shall possess their blessings. The dawn hour shall turn into showers of blessing and the cloud of Heaven shall shield them from the arrows of darkness, through their faith in Jesus and their obedience to God, in the name of Jesus. Amen.

Conclusion

All in all, Jesus Christ is Lord! We have started the race, and we have made it thus far! We've come to the end of this book, but the battle does not end here!

Knowledge of God's Word and dependence on His spirit are the keys to our liberty. I believe, with all my heart, that with this book, you will be able to unlock the freedom that you have always yearned for.

Going forward, I trust that as you walk through the prayers, ordained by God, through His servant, you will be able to experience deliverance, and be set apart to rule and reign in this life.

May God bless you as you walk in your new found blessings and peace. I thank God that through your faith in Jesus, and the help provided by this book, you have been delivered to possess your possession and to eternally enjoy the favor of God.

I hope that the Lord has touched your heart, and touched your mind with the words that were written therein. Let your path to deliverance start NOW! Let the love of Christ flow through YOU, NOW!

About the Author

Bishop R. W. Simmonds is the founder and presiding Bishop of Change Worship Ministries Int'l. He accepted the Lord at the age of 16, received his Bachelor of Arts in Theology in 2003 and was consecrated a Bishop in 2015.

Bishop Simmonds and his wife Pastor Claudette, of 34 years, have been blessed with three children and a granddaughter. He and his wife have had the privilege of working together in ministry and leading many souls to the Lord throughout the years of their service. They have seen many lives touched, impacted, changed and delivered through the working of The Holy Spirit. Bishop Simmonds' desire is to see God's people live an effective, complete, and delivered abundant life, and to be ready for eternity.

Trace Your Family Tree

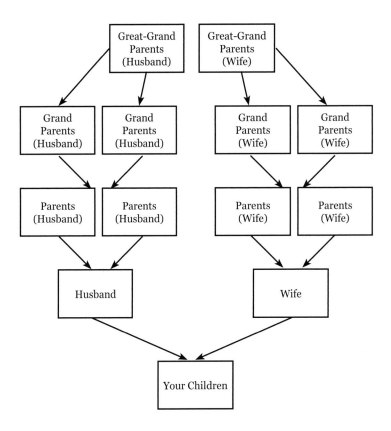

Please Note:
This is a sample of your family tree that the blessings or the curses flow through. Now that you have seen a family tree, I believe you can remove the tree of curse and be free to launch deep into the sea of success.

Notes

Notes

Notes

Notes